D1604646

Seventeenth in Bank Clearings Thirty Fourth City!

Farnam E. at 16th   Douglas W. at 16th   16th St. N. at Jackson   Douglas E. at 19th   Harney E. at 17th

Greetings from OMAHA Nebraska

Published by the

Omaha World-Herald
company

John Gottschalk, Chairman and President

ACKNOWLEDGEMENTS

Greetings from Omaha, Nebraska

Project Staff

Kristine Gerber, Co-Project Director
Paula Steenson, Co-Project Director
Jeffrey Spencer, Writer and Historian
Stacie Hamel, Copy Editor
Jen Hayduska, Project Assistant

Project Assistance

Murphy Benoit
Tam Falvo
Joe Sova
Dave Wuerfele

Book Production

Jacob North
Paula Presents!

Greetings from Omaha, Nebraska was a wonderful project. A special thanks to Burnice Fiedler for allowing us to share her postcard collection with all of you. We had many fun Fridays with Burnice looking through her extensive collection and hearing about her memories of Omaha.

Special effort was made to ensure the accuracy of the information for each postcard. However information written on the back of postcards is not always correct. For historical accuracy, we welcome corrected information, which we will forward to the appropriate archives and museums. Please send changes to the Omaha World-Herald, Marketing Department, World-Herald Square, Omaha, Nebraska 68102.

reetings From Omaha, Nebraska

Like miniature snapshots, early postcards
ture the visual essence of a community.
cards interest and intrigue us not only with
views themselves but also the story behind
pictures.

Collecting picture postcards is one of the
est growing hobbies in America, but
icated collectors also can be found in every
ntry of the world.

The science of postcard collecting — known
cially as deltiology – can be traced to Europe
he mid-19th century. The first view postcards
eared in Australia in 1869 and were of
ographic design. By 1870, they had made
ir debut in France. From those beginnings,
w postcards soon encompassed the world.

Modern picture postcards first were made
ilable in 1893 as result of the World's
umbian Exposition in Chicago, and the hobby
collecting postcards was born.

By 1906, 700 million postcards were being
d each year in America alone. By 1914, the
mber had climbed to 968 million cards. This
lains the large number of early cards that still
be found today.

The majority of cards issued during those
rs were chromo-lithographic cards. In this
cess a printed image, rather than a true
otographic image, was imprinted on the cards.
s was the principle method of card production
ween 1901 and 1907.

Postcards are commonly organized
according to seven eras:

- **Pioneer era,** 1893-1898
- **Private Mailing Card era,** 1898-1901
- **Postcard era,** 1901-1907
- **Divided Back era,** 1907-1915
- **White Border era,** 1915-1930
- **Linen era,** 1930-1945
- **Photochrome era,** 1939-present

Mailing cards were made possible in 1898
by a federal law allowing private printers to
produce and sell mailing cards. Cards produced
at this time had high-quality color printing and
an undivided back that allowed only for the
recipient's address. Messages were written on
the front.

In 1901, the words "Post Card" were allowed
to be printed on the reverse of the cards, for the
first time. Beginning in 1907, it was possible to
place both the address of the recipient and the
written message on the reverse of the card,
which had been divided into two equal spaces.

During World War I, the import of postcards
from Europe was suspended, and domestic
printing companies issued cards in America.
Generally, these "white-border cards" were of
poor quality.

Beginning in 1930, better paper and
improved printing techniques produced cards of
much higher quality.

"Chrome" cards, as they generally are
known, still dominate the postcard industry.

First introduced in 1939, they are distinguished
by bright, crisp colors and high-quality printing.
The view usually fills the card and allows no
"border."

Another type of postcard produced in great
quantities beginning in 1900 were real-photo
postcards. These photographs were printed onto
a postcard format. Photographic paper was
specially manufactured with postcard
designations printed on the reverse. Thus, an
amateur photographer could print and produce
his or her own photographic postcards. This
became an extremely popular venue, and large
quantities of these views still can be found today.

Prices in today's market are influenced by a
card's scarcity, condition and market demand.
Even so, with such large numbers of cards having
been produced, it still is possible to build an
interesting collection fairly quickly with a modest
investment.

In this book, we present to you a selection of
more than 400 views of scenes in and around
Omaha. Many of the locations and events
pictured no longer exist, and we have only these
images to remind us of these significant pieces of
our local history.

It gives us great pleasure to offer these views
for your enjoyment.

Jeffrey S. Spencer
Executive Director
Landmarks Inc.

TABLE OF CONTENTS

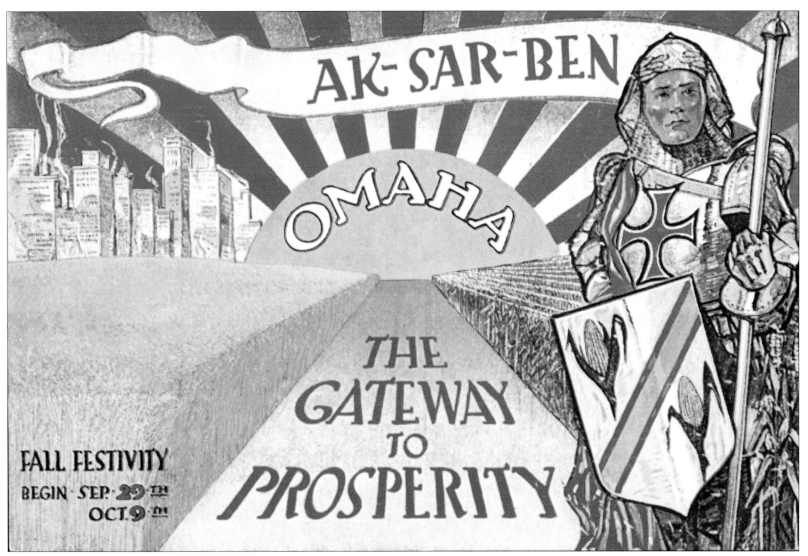

Ak-Sar-Ben Fall Festival in 1908

Ak-Sar-Ben street carnival in 1906

Ak-Sar-Ben parade float in 1913

Ak-Sar-Ben parade, passing 17th and Farnam Streets, in 1909

Ak-Sar-Ben parade float, 25th and Farnam Streets, in 1913

Ak-Sar-Ben parade float in 1916

Ak-Sar-Ben welcome arch, 17th and Farnam Streets, in 1920

Ak-Sar-Ben Rodeo participants, Ak-Sar-Ben field, 68th Street and Mercy Road, in 1920

Ak-Sar-Ben Rodeo at Ak-Sar-Ben field, 68th Street and Mercy Road, in 1925

Ak-Sar-Ben coronation at the Ak-Sar-Ben Coliseum, 20th and Burdette Streets, in 1925

Ak-Sar-Ben Coliseum, 68th Street and Mercy Road, in 1927

Ak-Sar-Ben Ball Room, 20th and Burdette Streets, in 1909

Aerial view of Ak-Sar-Ben Field and Coliseum, 68th Street and Mercy Road, in 19

Eve

...Sar-Ben Race Track and Grandstand, 68th Street and Mercy Road, in 1968

The Knights of Ak-Sar-Ben —

A community booster and benevolent association named by spelling Nebraska backwards, Ak-Sar-Ben was created in 1895 and has remained a major influence in the community. Each year, it sponsored a street carnival, electric parade and coronation ball. The group also funded community-improvement projects. Located first at the "Den" at 20th and Burdette Streets, the organization relocated in the 1920s to near 68th Street and Mercy Road, where a new coliseum and horseracing track were built.

National Corn Exposition

The National Corn Exposition was held in Omaha in December 1908 to focus attention on the agricultural potential of the Midwest. Gurdon Wattles, who served as president of the event, also had organized the Omaha Grain Exchange the same year. Held in the Omaha Auditorium at 15th and Howard Streets and in several annexes, the Corn Exposition attracted great interest. The 10-day event displayed a wide assortment of agricultural implements and exhibits on corn production. After the event's success, another exposition was held the next year, and hybrid seed corn was first introduced. The event was discontinued after the second year.

Eve

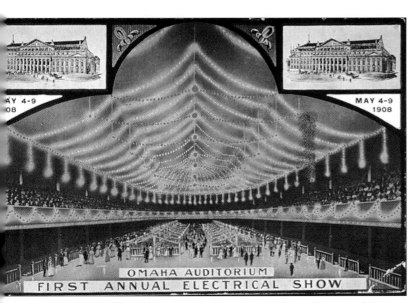

t Annual Electrical Show, Omaha Auditorium, 15th and Howard Streets, 908

Red Cross nurses in the "Kick the Kaiser" Parade, on Farnam Street downtown, in 1917

rman Day Parade in 1913

"Kick the Kaiser" Parade, 17th and Farnam Streets, in 1917

Seymour Guards Camp #16 on the roof of the Woodman of the World Building, 1319 Farnam St., in 1918

16th National Flower and Garden Show at the Omaha Auditorium, 15th and Howard Streets, in 1936

Official Seal and Emblem of the Omaha Centennial

Omaha Centennial Celebration in 1954

Eve

s-Mississippi and International Exposition horticulture building

Trans-Mississippi and International Exposition Boys and Girls building

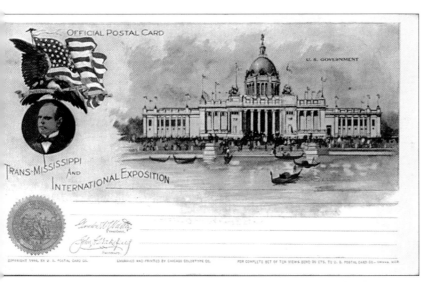

s-Mississippi and International Exposition U.S. Government building

The Trans-Mississippi and International Exposition and Indian Congress of 1898

This was, by far, the greatest event ever held in the city of Omaha.

An exposition company was formed to plan a great celebration for the summer of 1898. The idea first was introduced by William Jennings Bryan as a response to the economic hard times, which had dominated the Midwest since 1893. It was hoped that this great Exposition would ignite the local economy and attract attention from the country and the world.

Opening June 1, 1898, and running through Oct. 31 at 20th and Pinkney Streets, it was a great success, attracting 2.6 million visitors.

Mercer Hotel fire, northwest corner of 11th and Howard Streets, Jan. 28, 1905

Dewey Hotel fire, 312 S. 13th St., Feb. 28, 1913

Omaha Fires

Probably the most serious fire to occur in Omaha took place on Sept. 4, 1878 when the Grand Central Hotel burned. This large hotel was located on the southwest corner of 14th a Farnam Streets. The fire was the result of careless workmen who were repairing the interior. Five firemen were killed when the roof collapsed.

On Oct. 2, 1893, Omaha saw another fatal fire. The former Boyd's Opera House burne on Farnam Steet. A wall collapsed, injuring several persons and killing one fireman.

After the turn of the century, there were several spectacular fires, such as the Midland P and Glass Company at 16th and Harney Streets in 1903.

Jan. 28, 1905, saw the destruction of the Mercer Hotel at 11th and Howard Streets. A serious fire at the Woodman Linseed Oil Company on North 17th Street, occurred on Aug. of that same year.

Feb. 28, 1913, the Dewey Hotel (312 S. 13th St.) burned in a spectacular fire, and four persons were killed. The Omaha Board of Trade at 16th and Farnam Streets was destroyed Feb. 16, 1915.

The Armour Packing Company at 28th and Q Streets in South Omaha burned on Feb. 1 1923, and on June 24, 1927 the large Ak-Sar-Ben Den, at 20th and Burdette Streets was lost

er tornado destruction at Sacred Heart Academy (Duchesne), 36th and
oster Streets

Easter tornado, 36th and Burt Streets

er tornado, North 32nd Street

The Easter Tornado of March 23, 1913

The Easter Sunday tornado in 1913 became Omaha's greatest disaster.

Although Omaha had been in the path of other serious tornadoes — such as one in 1877 that destroyed the Union Pacific Railroad bridge across the Missouri River – the death toll never had been so high.

That Sunday, a tornado was seen about 6 p.m. approaching from the southwest. After destroying the community of Ralston, it moved into Omaha and first hit at 56th and Center Streets. It then moved northeast, through the main residential sections of the city.

The Gold Coast, Bemis Park and Dundee areas were heavily damaged. In all 3,179 homes were destroyed or damaged and about 100 people were killed.

ARCHITECTURE

Douglas Street, looking West, Omaha, Neb.

15th and Douglas Streets looking west in 1915

man Avenue Apartments, 2501 to 2509 N. 16th St., in 1907

Hamilton Apartments, 24th and Farnam Streets, in 1916

hlow Terrace, 2116 Sherman Ave., in 1915

Mount Vernon and Monticello Apartments, 520 S. 31st St., in 1930

Drake Court Apartments, 22nd and Jones Streets, in 1946

Rorick Apartments, 604 S. 22nd St., in 1958

Architect

second Nebraska Territorial Capitol building, 20th and Dodge Streets, in 1861

Federal Building and Post Office, 16th and Dodge Streets, in 1910

Omaha City Hall, 18th and Farnam Streets, in 1911

Omaha Water Works Minne Lusa Pumping Station, North 30th Street and Morman Bridge Road in Florence, in 1910

Douglas County Court House, 17th and Farnam Streets, in 1925

Bee Building and Omaha City Hall, 17th and Farnam Streets, in 1922

Omaha Architecture

The decade of the 1880s saw the transformation of Omaha fro wooden frame buildings to structures of brick and stone.

Prominent local architects such as Thomas R. Kimball and Joh Latenser designed many of Omaha's important structures. The m outstanding of these were the Post Office-Federal Building, constructed at 16th and Dodge Streets in the 1890s, and the New York Life Insurance Building at 17th and Farnam Streets in 1888.

Today, few of these early architectural examples remain, and v have only these photographic views to show us what has been los

Architect

No. 14. Exchange Building, Union Stock Yards, South Omaha, Nebraska.

ginal Livestock Exchange building, 29th and O Streets, in 1905

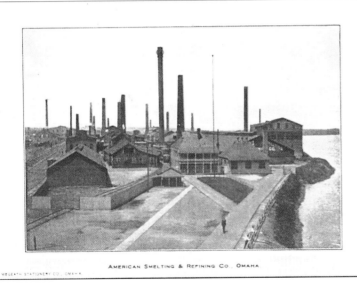

AMERICAN SMELTING & REFINING CO., OMAHA

MEGEATH STATIONERY CO., OMAHA

erican Smelting & Refining Co., Fifth and Dodge Streets, in 1905

No. 9. Nebraska Business College and Boyd Theatre, Omaha, Nebraska.

7/9/05.—

Sincerly Your

M. S. Rosenstadt

Nebraska Business College and Boyd Theatre, 1621
Harney St., in 1905

Omaha Grain Exchange building, 1901 to 1911 Harney St., in 1908

Stock Yards National Bank and Exchange building, 29th and O Streets, in 1908

Beaton Drug Co., 1501 Farnam St., in 1908

Architectu

tin Brothers Insurance Co., 15th and Farnam Streets, in 1908

mis Omaha Bag Co., 614 to 624 S. 11th St., in 1909

Conservative Savings and Loan Association, 1614 Harney St., in 1908

German Home, 4406 S. 13th St., in 1910

Byrne & Hammer Dry Goods Co., 9th and Howard Streets, in 1910

Murray Hotel and Paxton Hotel, 14th and Harney Streets, in 1910

Terminal Railway Warehouse Co., 702 S. 10th St., in 1912

Architectu

Woodman of the World building, 1319 Farnam St., in 1912

Omaha National Bank building, 17th and Farnam Streets, in 1915

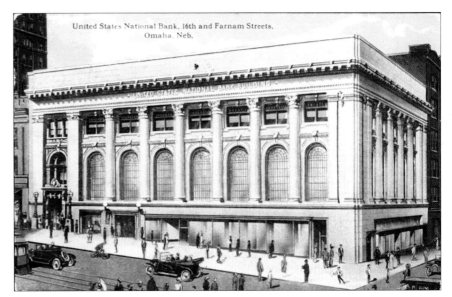

United States National Bank, 16th and Farnam Streets, in 1923

First National Bank, 1600 Farnam St., in 1923

Medical Arts building, 405 S. 17th St., in 1926

Northwestern Bell Telephone headquarters building, 19th and Douglas Streets, in 1918

Architectu

NATIONAL HEADQUARTERS BUILDING—SUPREME FOREST WOODMEN CIRCLE—OMAHA, NEBRASKA

...ional headquarters building of the Supreme Forest Woodmen Circle,
...d and Farnam Streets, in 1937

MUTUAL BENEFIT HEALTH AND ACCIDENT ASSOCIATION BUILDING, OMAHA, NEBRASKA

47993

Mutual Benefit Health and Accident Association building, 101 S. 36th St., in 1942

NEW BARKER BUILDING 15TH AND FARNAM STREET OMAHA NEBR

Barker building, 15th and Farnam Streets, in 1936

City National Bank building, 16th and Harney Streets, in 1951

Woodmen Tower, 17th and Farnam Streets, in 1970

Architect

ha wholesale district from 9th and Howard Streets in 1909

18th Street and Capitol Avenue looking west in 1909

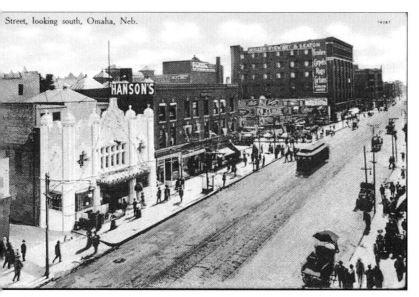

and Farnam Streets looking south in 1909

16th and Farnam Streets looking east in 1955

Guy C. Barton residence, 35th and Farnam Streets, in 1908

George A. Joslyn residence, 39th and Davenport Streets, in 1910

Arthur D. Brandeis residence, 38th Street and Dewey Avenue, in 1909

Ben Gallagher residence, 513 S. 38th St., in 1910

Architect

es along Lincoln Boulevard in Bemis Park, 33rd and Cuming Streets, in 1910

Arthur C. Storz residence, 3708 Farnam St., in 1970

Street and Woolworth Avenue looking toward Field Club in 1916

Gold Coast Area

At the end of the 19th Century, Omaha's population began to move away from the central city.

Prominent families began building large, elegant homes in the West Farnam neighborhood, an area from 33rd to 40th Streets and from Davenport to Jones Streets. This area was informally named "Omaha's Gold Coast" in reference to its large number of prosperous residents. One of the earliest homes was built in 1893 at 37th and Harney Streets by Gurdon Wattles, a prominent civic leader. Few of the homes remain today.

TRANSPORTATION

Entrance to Burlington Station, Omaha Neb.

THE BURLINGTON STATION

Burlington Station, 925 S. 10th St., in 1907

...aha's first street car built in 1866, pictured in 1924

Metz Brewery delivery wagon, 8th and Leavenworth Streets, in 1906

. Bennett Co. delivery wagon, 15th Street and Capitol Avenue, in 1905

Center Street Dairy delivery wagon in 1908

Gordon Fireproof Warehouse & Van Co., 11th and Davenport Streets, in 1915

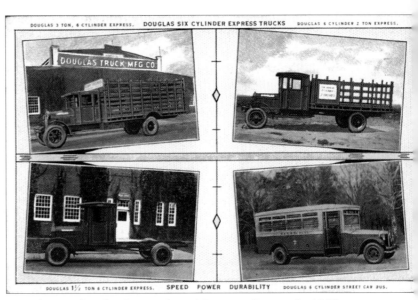

Douglas Truck Mfg. Co., 30th and Sprague Streets, in 1925

Curo Mineral Springs water delivery truck, offices at 1812 N St., in 1916

Andrew Murphy & Son, 1402 to 1420 Jackson St., in 1926

Transportat

...and Bros. Ashley Co., 1102 Farnam St., in 1909

Automobile Row, 20th to 22nd Street on Farnam, in 1921

...ce Clothing Co., 1323 Douglas St., in 1910

O.A. Olson & Son service station, 18th and Jackson Streets, in 1961

Burlington Station, 925 S. 10th St., in 1911

Burlington Station and the John J. Grier Co. News Stand, 925 S. 10th St., in 19

Burlington Station, 925 S. 10th St., in 1912

Chicago-Northwestern Railway freight terminal, 14th and Davenport Streets, in

Transporta

on Station, 10th and Marcy Streets, in 1908

Union Station, 10th and Marcy Streets, in 1910

on Station, 10th and Marcy Streets, in 1910

Union Station, 10th and Marcy Streets, in 1910

McKeen Motor Car, manufactured for Union Pacific Railroad at 1222 Webster St., in 1910

Union Pacific Railroad bridge, two blocks north of Pacific Street at the Missouri River, in 1904

Omaha Street Railway, 24th Street Crosstown car, in 1912

Ak-Sar-Ben Bridge, at foot of Douglas Street, between Omaha and Council Bluffs, in 1912

Transportat

142. O. Street Viaduct, South Omaha, Nebr.

...reet Viaduct in 1913

Illinois Central Railroad Bridge over the Missouri River between Omaha, Neb. and Council Bluffs, Iowa

Illinois Central Railroad bridge, east of Abbott Drive at Avenue H by Carter Lake, in 1925

U.S. AIR MAIL SERVICE

U.S. MAIL 605

U.S. AIRMAIL OMAHA NEBR.

Air Mail Service at Ak-Sar-Ben field, 68th Street and Mercy Road, in the 1920s

Municipal Airport and U.S. Weather Service Bureau in 1943

Martin B-26 Bomber, built at Martin Bomber Plant in Bellevue, in 1946

Overland Greyhound Bus Depot, 18th and Farnam Streets, in 1960

Transportation

Due to its strategic location, Omaha always has been an important transportation center. Missouri River steamboats gave way to railroa[d]s and by 1900 there were 11 railroads passing through and near Omaha. Many of these railroads had their own depots. The two most important, located along South 10th Street, were those of the Union Pacific and Burlington. Both were constructed in the late 1890s, in tim[e] to receive the many travelers who came to see the Exposition in 1898.

Burlington Station was especially outstanding. Designed by Thomas R. Kimball and completed in 1898, it was selected as one of the tw[o] most outstanding examples of Classic Revival architecture by the American Institute of Architects. By the 1880s, the street railway system w[as] transforming the city, making new neighborhoods possible. Hot-air balloons could be seen in Omaha beginning at the turn of the century, a[nd] the first plane was seen in 1909. Air transportation was first used at Ak-Sar-Ben Field, 68th Street and Mercy Road in the early 1920s. Soon after, Omaha built its first municipal airport on Abbott Drive.

DVERTISING

Brandeis Store, southwest corner of 16th and Douglas Streets, in 1919

Cudahy Packing Co., 33rd and O Streets, in 1894

Schlitz Roof Garden, 16th and Farnam Streets, in 1898

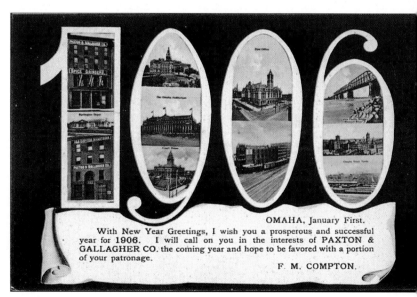

Paxton and Gallagher Co. in 1906

Adverti

ward Brothers Shoe Co., 1208 Howard St., in 1905

Campaign for Prohibition in Nebraska in 1910

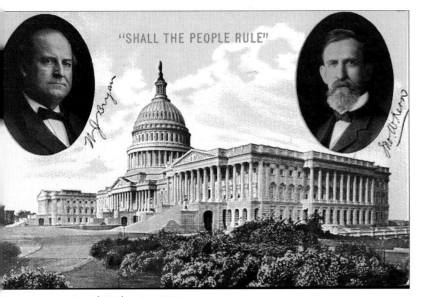

mocratic National Ticket in 1908

Hotel Fontenelle, 18th and Douglas Streets, in 1915

Benson & Thorne Clothing Co., 15th and Farnam Streets, in 1915

Members of the Omaha Municipal Court in 1942

Storz Brewing Co. delivery wagon in 1943

Adverti

Christiansen's Jewelry store in the fourth floor of the Securities Bldg., 16th & Farnam Streets, in 1958

United Airlines Halloween menu, Oct. 31, 1953

Glenn Cunningham for Congress in 1964

LORNA, NORBERT, MARY, AMY, LORNA, NORBERT, JR.

TIEMANN

NEBRASKA'S NEW WAY TO SPELL GOVERNOR

Norbert Tiemann for governor of Nebraska in 1968

He Cares!

The Thone family—Ann, Mary, Charley, Ruthie and Amy

☒ **CHARLES THONE**—Governor

Charles Thone for governor of Nebraska in 1972

Omaha Advertising

In the early 1900s, postcards were frequently used as advertising material. Direct-mail advertising did not exist then, and advertising in newspapers was rather limited. These types of cards were one of the most important advertising vehicles of the period.

RELIGIOUS INSTITUTIONS

Churches of Omaha in 1945

German Lutheran Church, located south of the old water tower in Millard, in 1891

Kountze Memorial Lutheran Church, 2602 Farnam St., in 1909

St. Agnes Catholic Church and parochial residence, 2211 Q St., in 1911

Religious Instituti

Sunday tabernacle built for an eight-week revival, 14th Street and Capitol Avenue, September and October 1915

First Swedish Baptist Church, 618 N. 18th St., in 1918

First Christian Church, 410 S. 26th St., in 1918

St. Philomena Catholic Church, 1334 S. 10th St., in 1918

Good Shepherd Convent, 653 S. 40th St., in 1922

Christian Science Church of Omaha, 24th Street and St. Mary's Avenue, in 1922

Central United Presbyterian Church, 102 N. 24th St., in 1925

Religious Instituti

Temple Israel.
Omaha, Neb.

ole Israel, 604 Park Ave., in 1925

FIRST BAPTIST CHURCH, OMAHA, NEB.   6540

Baptist Church, Park Avenue and Harney Street, in 1925

CHURCH OF SACRED HEART, 22ND AND BINNEY, OMAHA, NEB.

Church of the Sacred Heart, 22nd and Binney Streets, in 1925

gious Institutions

Sisters of Mercy Convent, 702 S. 27th St., in 1925

House of Hope (later the Florence Home), 7911 N. 30th St., in 1925

Pearl Memorial Methodist Church, 24th and Ogdon Streets, in 1927

Methodist Episcopal Church, 211 N. 20th St., in 1926

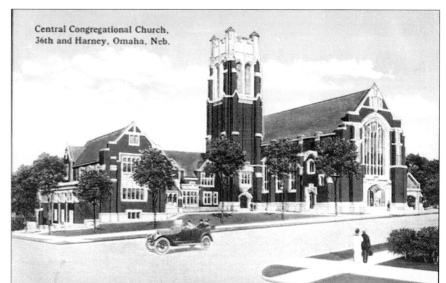

First Central Congregational Church, 36th and Harney Streets, in 1928

Mary Magdalene Catholic Church, 19th and Dodge Streets, in 1928

Our Lady of Lourdes Church and Rectory, 32nd Avenue and Frances Street, in 1930

St. Adalbert's Church and School, 2618 S. 30th St., in 1933

Omaha Gospel Tabernacle, 2006 Douglas St., in 1935

Immaculate Conception Church, 24th and Bancroft Streets, in 1934

Trinity Cathedral, 1719 Capitol Ave., in 1935

Religious Institutic

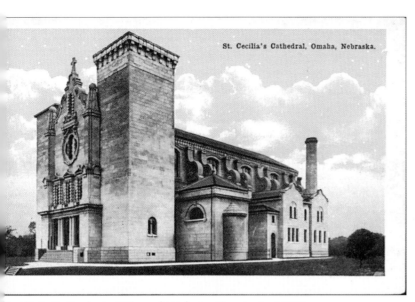

St. Cecilia's Cathedral, Omaha, Nebraska.

Cecilia's Cathedral, 40th and Webster Streets, in 1935

First Lutheran Church, 31st and Jackson Streets, in 1953

DUNDEE PRESBYTERIAN CHURCH
OMAHA, NEBRASKA

ndee Presbyterian Church, 55th Street and Underwood Avenue, in 1946

Religious Institutions

Omaha's first church building was St. Mary's Catholic Church, built at Ninth and Howard Streets in 1856. That same year, the Congregationalists built a small church on 16th Street, near Farnam.

The congregation of Temple Israel was organized in the 1870s, and its first synagogue was built in 1884 at 23rd and Harney Streets.

Construction began in 1907 on the great St. Cecilia's Cathedral at 40th and Webster Streets. This was architect Thomas Kimball's masterpiece.

LOCAL INSTITUTIONS

UNION STOCK YARDS, SHOWING EXCHANGE BUILDING, OMAHA, NEBR.

3001-29

Union Stockyards and Livestock Exchange Building, 29th and O Streets, in 1945

Edward J. Flanagan, founder of Father Flanagan's Boys Home (now Girls and Boys Town), in 1932

Father Flanagan's Boys' Home, Boys Town, Neb., in 1932

Father Flanagan's Boys' Home, Boys Town, Neb., in 1935

Boys Town in 1950

Boys Town

The internationally known Omaha institution, Girls and B[?] Town first opened its' doors Dec. 12, 1917.

Father Edward J. Flanagan, who at the time served as a pri[?] at St. Patrick's Church, had become concerned about homeless b[?] in Omaha. With initial financial assistance provided by an anonymous donor, he was able to secure an old home at 106 N. 25th St. This had been the former home of Byron Reed and was b[?] in 1875.

Soon, with 50 boys in residence, this location proved inadequate. A temporary move was made the next year to the forr[?] German-American Home, which had suspended activities as the result of anti-German feeling during World War I.

Later, a 40-acre farm in Florence was purchased. Then, as Flanagan's vision expanded, the Florence property was pledged a[?] down payment on the 160-acre "Overlook Farm" located 10 mile[?] west of Omaha in 1921. This is the present location of Girls and Boys Town.

Dowd Memorial Chapel, Boys Town, in 1950

Omaha Home For Boys, 52nd Street and Ames Avenue, in 1949

ames Orphanage, 60th Street and Radial Highway, in 1910

Bethlehem Children's Home, Immanuel Deaconess Institute, 34th Street and Fowler Avenue, in 1925

af and Dumb Institute, 45th Street and Bedford Avenue, in 1915

Child Saving Institute, 619 S. 42nd St., in 1958

Omaha General Hospital, 14th Street and Capitol Avenue, in 1908

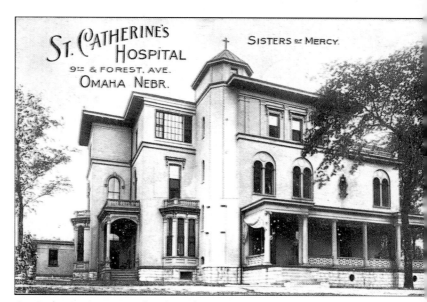

St. Catherine's Hospital, 9th and Forest Avenue, in 1912

Swedish Mission Hospital, 3706 N. 24th St., in 1911

Nazareth Home and Immanuel Hospital, 34th Street and Fowler Avenue, in 19

Local Institutio

...oathic Sanitorium, 2319 S. 13th St., in 1915

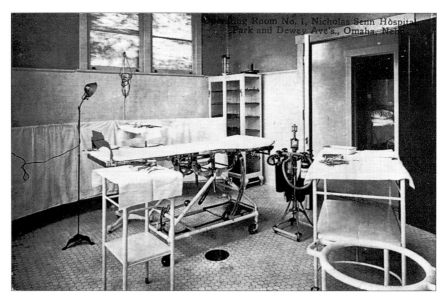

Nicholas Senn Hospital operating room, 501 Park Ave., in 1925

...d Lister Hospital waiting room, 14th Street and Capitol Avenue, in 1916

Methodist Episcopal Hospital, 36th and Cuming Streets, in 1925

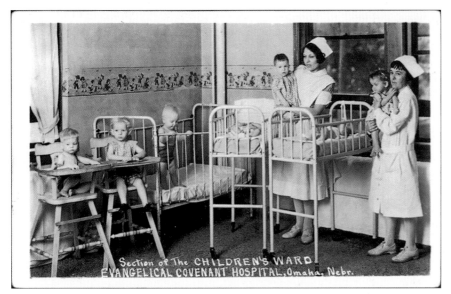

Evangelical Covenant Hospital Childrens Ward, 3706 N. 24th St., in 1931

Grotto of Creighton Memorial St. Joseph's Hospital, Omaha, Nebraska

St. Joseph's Hospital Grotto, 2205 S. 10th St., in 1935

St Joseph Hospital
Chapel
Omaha, Neb.

St. Joseph's Hospital Chapel, 2205 S. 10th St., in 1913

NEW DOUGLAS COUNTY HOSPITAL, OMAHA, NEBRASKA

Douglas County Hospital, 4102 Woolworth Ave., in 1937

Local Instituti

Children's Memorial Hospital, Omaha, Nebraska

dren's Memorial Hospital, 502 S. 44th St., in 1950

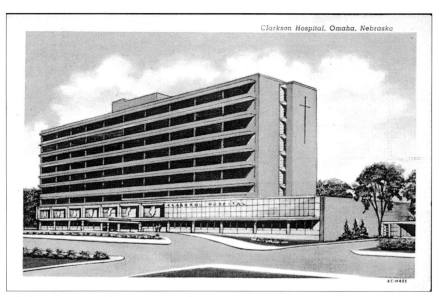

Clarkson Hospital, Omaha, Nebraska

Clarkson Memorial Hospital, 44th Street and Dewey Avenue, in 1956

raska Methodist Hospital lunch room, 36th and Cuming Streets, in 1950

Dr. G.D. Shipherd, Dentist, greeting his Patient Mr. Wm Peterson of Little Sioux Iowa, upon his arrival in Omaha. Dr. Shipherd sent this aeroplane to bring this patient to his new offices 613-20 Securities Bldg. 16th & Farnam Omaha

Dr. Shipherd (Omaha dentist with offices in the Security Building at 16th and Farnam Streets), in 1921

al Institutions

Lininger Art Gallery, 224 N. 18th St., in 1906

Strategic Air Command, Offutt Air Force Base in Bellevue, in 1955

Joslyn Memorial Art Museum, 2200 Dodge St., in 1955

Offutt Air Force Base, near Bellevue, in 1968

Local Instituti

Interior of Auditorium, Omaha, Neb.

aha Auditorium, 15th and Howard Streets, in 1907

SOKOL AUDITORIUM, 13TH AND MARTHA ST., OMAHA.

Sokol Auditorium, 13th and Martha Streets, in 1937

71. Auditorium, Omaha, Nebr.

maha Auditorium, 15th and Howard Streets, in 1910

OMAHA CIVIC AUDITORIUM

Omaha Civic Auditorium, 18th Street and Capitol Avenue, in 1955

YWCA, 508 S. 17th St., in 1912

WOW-TV, 3509 Farnam St., in 1951

YWCA gymnasium, 508 S. 17th St., in 1912

The Union Stockyards, 29th and O Streets, in 1954

Local Instituti

18. Soldiers Monument, Forest Lawn Cemetery, Omaha, Neb.

Grand Army of the Republic Soldiers Monument at Forest Lawn Cemetery, 7909 Morman Bridge Road, in 1920

"Winter Quarters" Mormon Cemetery, Northridge Drive and State Street, in 1951

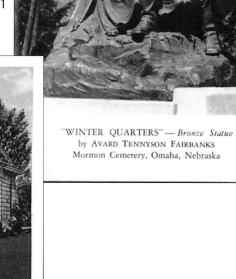

"WINTER QUARTERS" — *Bronze Statue* by AVARD TENNYSON FAIRBANKS Mormon Cemetery, Omaha, Nebraska

FOREST LAWN CHAPEL AND COLUMBARIUM, OMAHA, NEBRASKA

Chapel and Columbarium, Forest Lawn Cemetery, 7909 Morman Bridge Road, in 1940

ENTERTAINMENT & RECREATION

Famous Royal Grove—Peony Park. looking from the Bandstand

Famous Royal Grove—Peony Park. looking from the Fountain Stand

Peony Park's Royal Grove, 8100 Cass St., in 1948

Peony Park's Royal Terrace, 8100 Cass St., in 1943

Peony Park

Joseph Malec, Sr., first opened a refreshment stand on property along the Papio Creek in west Omaha in 1919. By 1921, this business had expanded to include a restaurant, named the "Peony Inn." Additional attractions were added and eventually the name was changed to "Peony Park." The new name was derived from the "Peony Gardens," a large peony farm which was located across the street.

A swimming pool open in 1926, and in the early 1930s an outdoor dancing area, the Royal Grove, was added. This attracted many of the important big bands of the day and was a very popular entertainment spot in Omaha.

In 1958, amusement rides were added and by 1968 it included 19 different rides.

The park was closed in the late 1980s. In 1994 it was placed in receivership and dismantled.

Peony Park's Royal Terrace, 8100 Cass St., in 1952

Peony Farm, 78th and Cass Streets, in 1910

Omaha Philharmonic Orchestra in 1905

Golden Prague Orchestra featured on radio station WAAW in 1937

The Menoma Chorus at Brandeis Theatre April 19, 1917

Featured performers on the Union Pacific Railroad radio show "Your America," in 1952

Entertainment & Recreat

WOW radio personality "Aunt Sally" in 1955

Burwood Theatre, Omaha, Neb.

No. 212. Omaha Souvenir and Novelty Co., Omaha, Neb.

Burwood Theatre, 1514 Harney St., in 1906

Boyd's Theatre, 17th and Harney Streets, in 1906

Brandeis Theatre, 212 S. 17th St., in 1906

American Music Hall, 18th and Douglas Streets, in 1912

Riviera Theatre, 20th and Farnam Streets, in 1921

era Theatre, 20th and Farnam Streets, in 1921

OMAHA'S FINEST PLAYHOUSE. WORLD THEATRE. OMAHA, NEBR.

World Theatre, 1506 Douglas St., in 1927

RIALTO THEATRE, 15TH AND DOUGLAS STREETS, OMAHA, NEBR.

to Theatre, 1424 Douglas St., in 1926

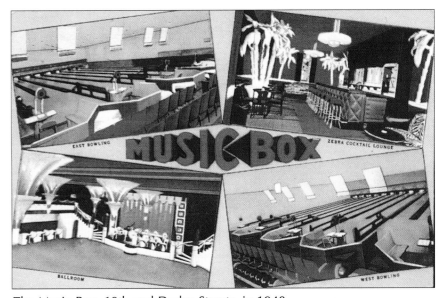

The Music Box, 19th and Dodge Streets, in 1948

Indian Hills Theatre, 8601 West Dodge St., in 1964

Carter Lake Club House in 1908

Omaha Community Playhouse, 6915 Cass St., in 1965

Carter Lake in 1912

Entertainment & Recreati

Yachting on Lake Nakoma off the Missouri River between Omaha and Council Bluffs in 1910

Bathers in the Sand, Lake Manawa, Iowa.

Lake Manawa in 1911

"WHERE WE USED TO BATHE"
CUT OFF LAKE, OMAHA, NEB.

Cut Off Lake, off the Missouri River between Omaha and Council Bluffs, in 1909

Courtland Beach, Omaha, Neb.

Courtland Beach at Cut Off Lake, off the Missouri River between Omaha and Council Bluffs, in 1913

Entertainment & Recreation

Yacht Racing at Lake Manawa in 1920

Jefferson Square Park, North 15th Street between Chicago and Cass Streets, in

Merritt Beach, at the Platte River Bridge, in 1955

Krug Park, 52nd Street and Military Avenue, in 1909

Entertainment & Recreati

Krug Park, 52nd Street and Military Avenue, in 1915

Elmwood Park Pavilion, 60th and Leavenworth Streets, in 1910

Elmwood Park's bridge and spring, 60th and Leavenworth Streets, in 1910

Elmwood Park's Monkey Island, 60th and Leavenworth Streets, in 1936

Birch Drive in Miller Park, 6100 N. 24th St., in 1911

Bemis Park, 33rd and Cuming Streets, in 1912

Entertainment & Recrea

Riverview Park Pavilion, 3500 S. Ninth St., in 1911

Riverview Park Lake, 3500 S. Ninth St., in 1912

Riverview Park buffalo, 3500 S. Ninth St., in 1915

Seymour Park, 74th and Q Streets in Ralston, in 1910

Lake Manawa Pavilion in 1922

Syndicate Park (later part of Riverview Park), 3625 S. 10th St., in 1916

Kountze Park, North 19th and 21st Streets at Pinkney Street, in 1925

Entertainment & Recrea

Hanscom Park Pavilion. Omaha, Nebr.

com Park Pavilion, 1501 S. 32nd Ave., in 1907

SOUTH RIVER DRIVE TO MANDAN PARK, OMAHA, NEBR.

Mandan Park, 6215 S. 13th St., in 1930

CONSERVATORY AND FLOWER BEDS, HANSCOM PARK. OMAHA, NEBR.

com Park's Conservatory and Flower Beds, 1501 S. 32nd Ave., in 1925

Fontenelle Forest, Wild Life Sanctuary, near Omaha, Neb.

Fontenelle Forest Wild Life Sanctuary, Bellevue Boulevard, in 1943

Mount Vernon Gardens, 5849 S. 13th St., in 1943

John J. Pershing Memorial and Pershing Memorial Drive, 6500 N. Nint in 1950

Benson Park Lagoon and Pavilion, 7088 Military Ave., in 1947

Curtis Turner Park, 30th and Dodge Streets, in 1951

Entertainment & Recrea

Club House, Fontenelle Park, Omaha, Neb.

nelle Park Club House, 4400 Fontenelle Blvd., in 1952

World War II Memorial Park, Omaha, Nebraska

World War II Memorial at Memorial Park, 55th and Dodge Streets, in 1954

DEWEY PARK TENNIS CENTER
OMAHA, NEBRASKA

ey Park Tennis Center, 550 Turner Blvd., in 1954

Playland Park
"The Amusement Center of Omaha and Council Bluffs"

Playland Park Roller Coaster, east end of the Ak-Sar-Ben Bridge at Douglas Street in Council Bluffs, in 1956

EDUCATION

BOYLES COLLEGE, OMAHA, NEB.

BOYLES-COLLEGE

Boyles College, 1805 Harney St., in 1907

son Central High School, 63rd and Maple Streets, in 1906

Omaha Commercial College, 1824 Farnam St., in 1906

yles College students in front of the YMCA, 1707 Harney St., in 1919

ucation

Creighton University's main wing, 24th and California Streets, in 1908

Aerial view of Creighton University, 24th and California Streets, in 1938

St. John Church at Creighton College, 24th and California Streets, in 1915

Creighton University's Administration Building, 24th and California Streets, in 1

Educa

rict #27 High School, Halleck and Adams Streets in Papillion, in 1912

Brownell Hall school, 10th and Worthington Streets, in 1914

rence High School, 8516 N. 31st. St., in 1914

Chambers Dancing Academy, 2424 Farnam St., in 1915

ucation

Omaha High School, 124 N. 20th St., in 1915

Academy of the Sacred Heart, 3601 Burt St., in 1926

Presbyterian Theological Seminary, 3303 N. 21st St., in 1925

Notre Dame Academy, 3501 State St., in 1930

Educati

Municipal University, 60th and Dodge Streets, in 1940

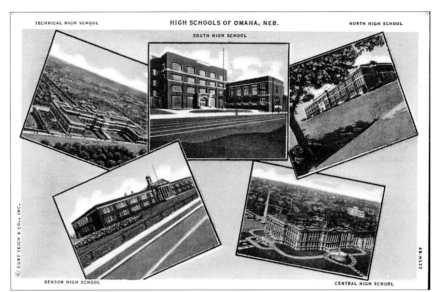

Omaha High Schools in 1950

California School of Beauty, 521 N. 33rd St., in 1941

Grace Bible Institute, 1515 S. 10th St., in 1955

A Kiss from Everybody in Omaha, Neb.

OMAHA GREETINGS

Omaha Greeting in 1912

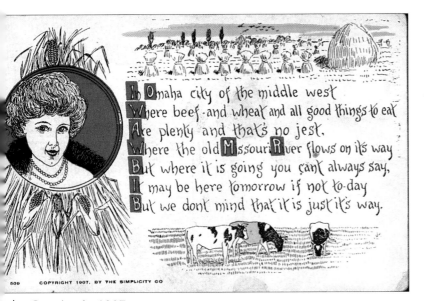

In **O**maha city of the middle west
Where beef and wheat and all good things to eat
Are plenty and that's no jest,
Where the old **M**issouri **R**iver flows on its way
But where it is going you can't always say,
It may be here tomorrow if not to-day
But we don't mind that it is just it's way.

509   COPYRIGHT 1907, BY THE SIMPLICITY CO.

aha Greeting in 1907

PAPILLION, NEB.

6121

Papillion Greeting in 1911

GREETINGS from OMAHA
1907

naha Greeting in 1907

OH! WHAT FUN WE HAD
In Omaha, Neb.

THE BIG SHOW

RIDE 5¢

Omaha Greeting in 1913

maha Greetings

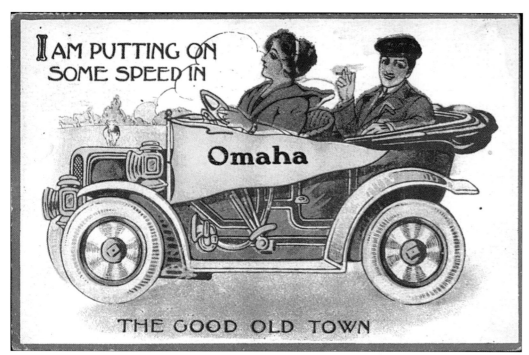

Omaha Greeting in 1913

Omaha Greeting in 1913

Omaha Greetir

EVERYBODY'S HAPPY
At OMAHA

...ha Greeting in 1914

Bird's Eye View of Wholesale District,
Omaha, Neb.

Aerial View of the wholesale district, along the Missouri front, east of the retail district, in 1922

Greetings From
OMAHA, NEBRASKA

You've doubtless heard of other
towns
That have some "push"
and "snap"
But the place I mail this card
from
Is the "Best Town on
the Map."

Omaha Greeting poem in 1913

Fort Crook Greetings in 1950

Omaha at Night, downtown 16th Street, in 1952

ha Greeting featuring area landmarks in 1960

Greeting from Ak-Sar-Ben in 1967

l view of the Missouri River and downtown Omaha in 1965

Downtown Omaha in 1968

OMAHA ATHLETIC CLUB, OMAHA, NEBR.

Omaha Athletic Club, 1714 Douglas St., in 1925

Omaha Club, 20th and Douglas Streets, in 1908

Rod and Gun Club, Lake Manawa, in 1909

Eagles Hall, 6205 Maple St., October 1908

Rod and Gun Club Skippers, Lake Manawa, in 1910

Field Club, 36th Street and Woolworth Avenue, in 1910

South Omaha Country Club, South 13th Street, in 1912

Private Clubs

The business and social elite of Omaha established private clubs, such as the Omaha Country Club in 1899 in the present-day Benson-Country Club area. The Omaha Club began in 1884, with an initial membership of 245. Part of the Happy Hollow Club at 55th Street and Underwood Avenue became the site of Brownell Hall and later Brownell-Talbot school.

Field Club, 36th Street and Woolworth Avenue, in 1910

Florence Masonic Temple in 1914

Arab Patrol, Tangier Temple, 1608 Capitol Ave., in 1915

Legionnaire Club, 1818 Farnam St., in 1943

Seymour Lake Country Club, 74th and Q Streets in Ralston, in 1916

Happy Hollow Club, 55th Street and Underwood Avenue, in 1925

Knights of Columbus Club, 2025 Dodge St., in 1925

Camp Brewster, Bellevue Boulevard, in 1935

Private Cl

TOWER TOURIST VILLAGE — 78th and DODGE STREET — OMAHA, NEBRASKA

LOCATED ON HIGHWAYS NO. 30A, 6, 275 AND 92.

Tower Tourist Village, 78th and Dodge Streets, in 1953

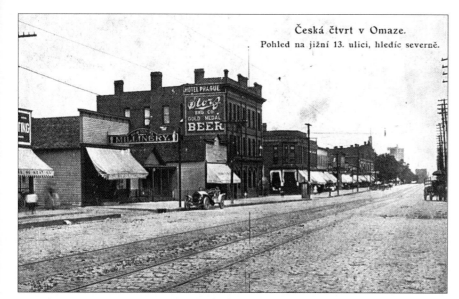

Hotel Prague, 13th and William Streets, in 1906

Paxton Hotel, 14th and Farnam Streets, in 1908

Hotel Loyal, 215 N. 16th St., in 1908

Merriam Hotel, 106 S. 25th St., in 1901

Commercial Establishments & Busines

Millard Hotel, Omaha, Neb.
European.
Cor. 13th and Douglas Sts.

Popular Priced Cafe.
Finest in City.

Millard Hotel, 13th and Douglas Streets, in 1910

Hotel Rome, European, Omaha, Neb.
Cor. 16th and Jackson Streets.
Rome Miller.

Hotel Rome, 16th and Jackson Streets, in 1915

Hotel Sanford, Omaha, Neb.

Hotel Sanford, 19th and Farnam Streets, in 1911

HOTEL
ROME
OMAHA

Unexcelled in the West
for its beauty and
modern appointments.
ROME MILLER

Hotel Rome, 16th and Jackson Streets, in 1915

Hotel Omaha, 516 S. 16th St., in 1915

Carlton Hotel, 15th and Howard Streets, in 1916

Hotel Castle, 628 to 632 S. 16th St., in 1915

Drexel Hotel, 618 N. 16th St., in 1916

Commercial Establishments & Busines

Grand Hotel, 16th and Howard Streets, in 1916

el Edward, 16th and Davenport Streets, in 1917

Slogr Hotel & Restaurant, 1431 S. 13th St., in 1917

Hotel Conant, 16th and Harney Streets, in 1918

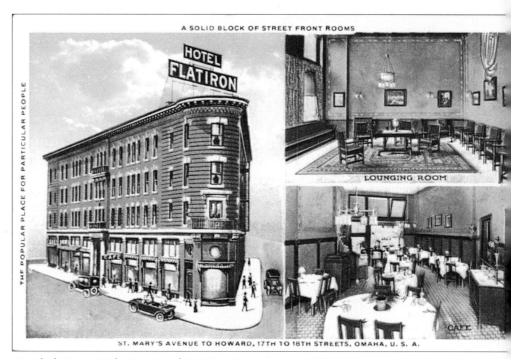

Hotel Flatiron, 17th Street and St. Mary's Avenue, in 1915

Blackstone Hotel Ball Room, 36th and Farnam Streets, in 1918

Blackstone Hotel dining room, 36th and Farnam Streets, in 1918

Blackstone Hotel Main Lobby, 36th and Farnam Streets, in 1916

The Blackstone Hotel, 36th and Farnam Streets, in 1920

7621.
The Henshaw Hotel,
Omaha, Neb.

The Henshaw Hotel, 1509 to 1515 Farnam St., in 1911

Hotel Harney, (European)
Chas. C. Sorensen, Prop,
14th and Harney Streets,
Omaha, Nebr.

Hotel Harney, 14th and Harney Streets, in 1922

Commercial Establishments & Busines

Hotel Hill, 506 S. 16th St., in 1925

D. L. D. Modern Heated Cabin Camp

"A Home on the Highway"   Ask the Man That Stayed There

| 6323 Center Street | OMAHA | 2 blocks west of City Limits |
| U. S. Highway No. 6, State Highway No. 16 | | South of AK-SAR-BEN Field |

Phone Walnut 0122   Open Year Round

D.L.D. Modern Heated Cabin Camp, 6323 Center St., in 1945

Blue Arrow Motel, intersection of U.S. Highways 6 and 30, in 1950

Indian Hills Trailer Park, 87th and Dodge Streets, in 1955

Dillon Drug Store, 902 N. 16th St., in 1909

Owl Drug Store, 16th and Harney Streets, in 1908

Carl S. Baum Drug Store in The Center Mall, 42nd and Center Streets, in 19

Commercial Establishments & Busines

Old Age Buffet, 314 S. 14th St., in 1910

The Empress Garden Restaurant, 1514 Douglas St., in 1921

umet Restaurant Annex, 1411 to 1413 Douglas St., in 1912

Giovanni's Round Table, 19th and Harney Streets, in 1950

Dixon's Cafe and Cocktail Lounge, 18th and
Farnam Streets, in 1941

Sam Nisi's Spare Time Cafe, 1211 S. Fifth St., in 1951

r's Drive Inn Restaurant, junction of Highways 6 and 92, in 1952

Ross' Steak House, 909 S. 72nd St., in 1955

top House, 49th and Dodge Streets, in 1952

The Fountain Room in Kiewit Plaza, 36th and Farnam Streets, in 1960

Bishop Buffet at the Westroads Shopping Center, 102nd Street and West Dodge Road, in 1968

Commercial Establishments & Busines

len Brothers, 104 to 112 S. 16th St., in 1907

DO YOU KNOW ?
BENNETT'S CAFE
SERVES A
50c TABLE D'HOTE
DINNER
EVERY SATURDAY
EVENING,
5:30 TO 8

MUSIC BY
Kaufman's Orchestra

Cafe open every day—8 A. M. to 5:30 P.M.
Cuisine unexcelled.   Popular prices.

The Bennett Company

The Bennett Co., 16th and Harney Streets, in 1904

len Brothers, 104 to 112 S. 16th St., in 1911

*This is The Store that
sets the pace*
LOW PRICES are the
cause of our popularity

*Correct Dress for
Nen and Boys*
BERG CLOTHING CO.
15 & Douglas Sts. Omaha.

Berg Clothing Co., 15th and Douglas Streets, in 1910

Boston Store (later became the Brandeis Store), 16th and Douglas Streets, in 1905

Brandeis Store, southwest corner of 16th and Douglas Streets, in 1912

Main floor of the Brandeis Store, southwest corner of 16th and Douglas Streets, in 1912

Commercial Establishments & Busine

ond floor of the Brandeis Store, southwest corner of 16th and Douglas
ets, in 1910

ndeis Store display, southwest corner of 16th and Douglas Streets, in 1914

Brandeis Store, southwest corner of 16th and Douglas Streets,
December 1908

mmercial Establishments & Businesses

Burgess-Nash Co., 16th and Harney Streets, in 1915

C.B. Brown Co. Jewelers, 220 S. 16th St., in 1922

Brodegaard Bros. Co. Jewelers, 16th and Douglas Streets, in 1925

Woolworth's Store, 16th and Douglas Streets, in 1955

Commercial Establishments & Busines

Center Shopping Center, 42nd and Center Streets, in 1958

Westroads Shopping Center, 102nd Street and West Dodge Road, in 1968

Crossroads Shopping Center, 72nd and Dodge Streets, in 1965

J.S. Cross Saloon, 1402 Douglas St., in 1909

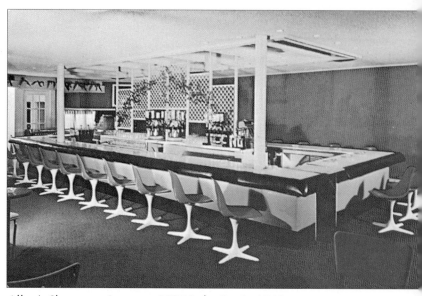

Allen's Showcase Lounge, 2229 Lake St., in 1960

Little Frank's Tavern, 2918 N. 16th St., in 1934

Commercial Establishments & Business

Western Electrical Co., 411 to 413 S. 10th St., in 1907

Live Stock National Bank, 24th and N Streets, in 1908

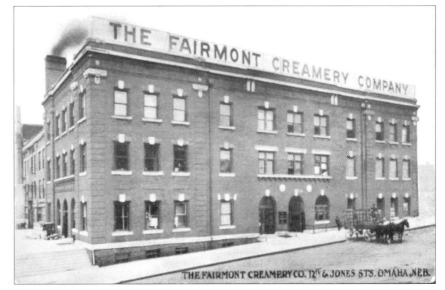

The Fairmont Creamery Co., 12th and Jones Streets, in 1909

411-413 SO. TENTH ST.   OMAHA, NEB.

Omaha Tent & Awning Co.,
Omaha, Neb.

Omaha Tent & Awning Co., 1023 Harney St., in 1908

Independent Lumber Company, 3912 to 3923 Leavenworth St., in 1908

Benson business district, 61st and Maple Streets looking west, in 1908

Commercial Establishments & Business

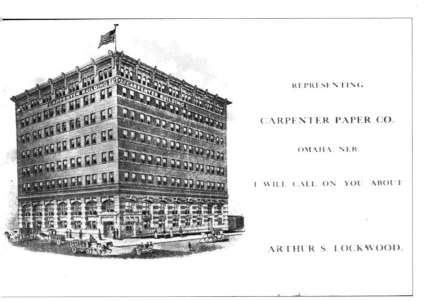

REPRESENTING

CARPENTER PAPER CO.

OMAHA, NEB.

I WILL CALL ON YOU ABOUT

ARTHUR S. LOCKWOOD.

Carpenter Paper Co., 1118 to 1124 Howard St., in 1908

Omaha Printing Co., 1301 Farnam St., in 1909

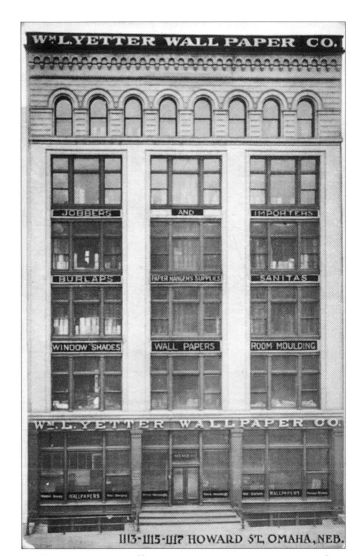

William L. Yetter Wallpaper Co., 1113 to 1117 Howard St., in 1909

Commercial Establishments & Businesses

Sherman Ave. Meat and Produce Market, 2909 to 2911 Sherman Ave., in 1909

Clay, Robinson & Co. Room 299 in the Livestock Exchange Building, 29 and O Streets, in 1910

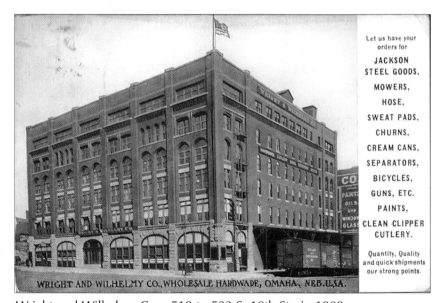

Wright and Wilhelmy Co., 519 to 523 S. 10th St., in 1909

Omaha Paper Box Co., 1423 Leavenworth St., in 1910

Commercial Establishments & Busines

ha Casket Co., 1618 Izard St., in 1908

The Alfred Bloom Co., 15th and California Streets, in 1910

aha Fireproof Storage Co., 806 S. 16th St., in 1910

McClure's Cash Store, North 30th Street, Florence business district, in 1911

mmercial Establishments & Businesses

Brown Truck Manufacturing Co., 75th and Burlington Streets in Ralston, in 1911

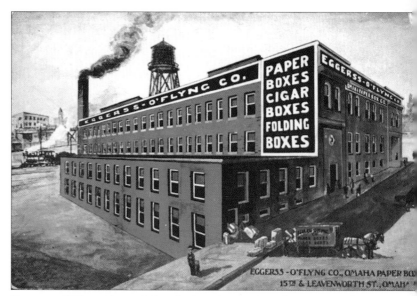

Eggerss - O'Flyng Co. and Omaha Box Co., 15th and Leavenworth Streets, in

Omaha News Co., 15th and Davenport Streets, in 1912

Roller Mills, along Papio Creek in Papillion, in 1912

Commercial Establishments & Business

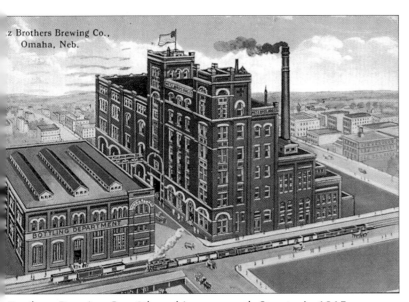

Brothers Brewing Co., 8th and Leavenworth Streets, in 1915

Storz's Brewing Co., Omaha, Neb.

Storz Brewing Co., 1819 Sherman Ave., in 1908

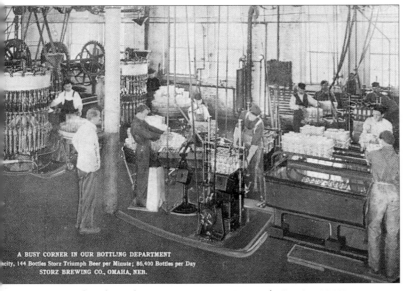

A BUSY CORNER IN OUR BOTTLING DEPARTMENT
acity, 144 Bottles Storz Triumph Beer per Minute; 86,400 Bottles per Day
STORZ BREWING CO., OMAHA, NEB.

Brewing Co. bottling department, 1819 N. 16th St., in 1915

The Rose Building and Henshaw Hotel, 16th & Farnum Sts., Omaha, Neb.

The Rose Building and Henshaw Hotel, 16th and Farnam Streets, in 1916

Skinner Macaroni plant, 14th and Jackson Streets, in 1918

Commercial Savings and Loan Association, Philbins Barber Shop and O'Neil's Real Estate & Insurance Agency, 1505 Farnam St., in 1928

Alamito Dairy, 26th and Leavenworth Streets, in 1915

Haarmann Vinegar and Pickle Co., 12th and Marcy Streets, in 1922

Commercial Establishments & Busine

THE BANKERS RESERVE LIFE BUILDING
OMAHA. - - NEBR.

Bankers Reserve Life Building, 1613 Farnam St., in 1921

Hulse and Riepen Funeral Home, 33rd and Farnam Streets, in 1930

BURNICE FIEDLER

Almost from the day she was born in Omaha in 1917, Burnice Beal Fiedler has been a student of this city's history and a collector of i memories. Through the years, she has assisted historians, writers and educators as they sought information on Omaha's history. Now she i helping all of us catch a glimpse of bygone Omaha through this book. The images you see in "Greetings from Omaha, Nebraska" represe only a small portion of what is, without question, the finest and most complete collection of Omaha postcards.

Burnice Fiedler's "Omaha collection" contains more than 20,000 postcards. She also has collected tens of thousands of other postcard covering a range of topics.

Burnice hopes that all that view this book will experience some of the joy and interest she experienced as she assembled this remarka collection. It would be virtually impossible to duplicate this collection, as so many of the views now are extremely rare, if not unique. If y were to ask Burnice when she started collecting, she probably would tell you she has been doing that most of her life. Her collecting hob became more serious in the late 1950s when she became interested in coins. After the collapse of the silver market in the late '70s and ea '80s, Burnice's emphasis shifted to collecting postcards.

While growing up in Omaha, Burnice attended what was then Saunders Elementary School, at 41st and Cass Streets and Technical Hig School at 30th and Cuming Streets. After graduation in 1935, she went to work for Matthew's Book Store, which was at 15th and Harney Streets, and later for the O'Brien Drug Company at 17th and Douglas Streets. She worked for O'Brien's for 50 years.

Burnice was married to Howard Fiedler on March 7, 1942, in Omaha. Soon after their wedding, Howard went overseas to serve in th Army during World War II.

Along with her interest in the local community, Burnice has been supportive of many historical organizations. She played a major rol the development of the Trans-Mississippi Exposition Historical Association, founded in 1990. This involvement was the direct result of an of her collecting interests: material from the great Trans-Mississippi and International Exposition held in Omaha during the summer of 189

Burnice would tell you that she was assisted by many others while building her collection, including her friends Elaine Swanson, Dear Wittstruck and Pat Loeck, as well as her niece Helen Edwards and husband David. Of all her extensive collections, Burnice would tell you her collection of friends that she holds most dear.

Thank you Burnice for also being a friend to Omaha by sharing these wonderful views with all of us.

Burnice Fiedler

40th Anniversary of Beal's Grill, 24th and California Streets in 1980

Display of material from Beals Grill at Creighton University Student Center in 1986

127

Panoramic view of Omaha looking east on Capitol Avenue from 20th Street in 1908